This book has been published in cooperation with Evans Publishing Group.

© Evans Brothers Limited 2010
This edition published under license from Evans Brothers Limited.

Published in the United States by
Amicus
P.O. Box 1329, Mankato, Minnesota 56002

Printed in China by New Era Printing Co.Ltd

Library of Congress Cataloging-in-Publication Data

Barker, Geoff P., 1963-
  Health and social care careers / by Geoff Barker.
    p. cm. -- (In the workplace)
  Summary: "Describes jobs in the medical and social care fields. Includes information
on doctors, nurses, and social workers, and their responsibilities"--Provided by publisher.
  Includes index.
  ISBN 978-1-60753-091-6 (lib. bdg.)
  1. Medical personnel--Vocational guidance--Popular works. 2. Allied health personnel--Vocational guidance--Popular
works. 3. Human services personnel--Vocational guidance--Popular works. I. Title.
  R690.B37 2011
  610.69023--dc22

                                                                2009045302

Editor and picture researcher: Patience Coster
Designer: Guy Callaby

The author would like to thank the following for their help in producing this book: April Adam and Caroline; Pete
Collin; Caroline Georgiou; Tyler Gonzalez; Alice Hall; Berenice Holder; Michelle Jordan; May Mackenzie; Anne Maiden
and Shirley Black; Dilip Mistry; Jenny Pocock; Katrina Preston; Scott Rintoul; David Thompson.

We are grateful to the following for permission to reproduce photographs: Alamy 6 (Picture Partners), 7 (Angela
Hampton Picture Library), 8 (Jochen Tack), 9 (G. P. Bowater), 12 (Mike Abrahams), 13 (Janine Wiedel Photolibrary), 14
(Bill Bachmann), 17 (David Taylor), 20 (Joel Wintermantle), 21 (Mira), 22 (Janine Wiedel Photolibrary), 23 (Janine
Wiedel Photolibrary), 25 (Photofusion Picture Library), 26 (Caro), 27 (Paul Doyle), 28 (Mike Goldwater), 29
(walespix), 30 (Angela Hampton Picture Library), 33 (Paul Doyle), 35 (Martin Mayer), 36 (Paula Solloway), 38
(Bubbles Photolibrary), 39 (Janine Wiedel Photolibrary), 40 (Janine Wiedel Photolibrary), 41 (Jack Sullivan), 42
(Photofusion Picture Library), 43 (Bubbles Photolibrary); Corbis 10 (Ed Kashi), 11 (John Henley), 15 (Chad Ehlers –
Stock Connection/Science Faction), cover and 16 (Ed Kashi), 31 (Ann Johansson), 32 (Tom Stewart); Getty Images 18
(David Harry Stewart), 24 (Charles Gupton), 34 (Andrew Bret Wallis); Science Photo Library 19 (Sean O'Brien,
Custom Medical Stock Photo).

05 10
PO1568

9 8 7 6 5 4 3 2 1

DATE DUE

DEC 1 5 2021	JAN 2 6 2022

DEMCO, INC. 38-2931

IN THE
WORKPLACE

Health AND Social Care Careers

GEOFF BARKER

amicus
mankato, minnesota

Contents

Working in Health and Social Care

The health care and social work sector concerns the health and well-being of people in the community. For many of us, the most familiar aspect of health and social care will be the doctor's office, where we go when we feel sick and need treatment. But during the course of our lives, on those occasions when we need help with our physical or our mental health, we may encounter many other people working in this very important area.

CARING FOR OTHERS

If you are interested in working in health and social care, a huge range of jobs are open to you. This book shows a sample of the careers available, from that of doctor, nurse, or midwife to child and youth services, which concern the welfare and development of younger people on the path to adulthood. For example, child social workers offer help to young children and teenagers who have troubled home lives. They work with the young people, their parents, and their educators to ensure they get the services and stability they need to have a chance at success in their education, relationships, and life in general.

HEALTH CARE

When patients suffer from illnesses, their condition is often first diagnosed by a doctor. They may then be referred to a health specialist. They will be treated and hopefully will make a quick and full recovery, or they may need some sort of rehabilitation or adjustment to their lifestyle. If the condition is ongoing, they may need to see a number of health professionals on a regular basis. For example, a diabetic adult may visit a doctor, nurse, optician, or optometrist. He or she may even visit a specialized diabetes clinic.

A midwife wraps a newborn baby. Midwives play a vitally important role for the family and in the community.

Health care workers need to be professional, dedicated, patient, and hardworking. They should also have good communication skills and a genuine interest in their patients. Work can be difficult and stressful when patients are weak and vulnerable, and especially when hours are long. However, working in this sector can be extremely rewarding. There are few jobs that deal so closely and intimately with real issues of life, from birth to death. If you're looking for a career in this field, you need to be mentally tough as well as compassionate. If you think you want to be a nurse but are squeamish and faint at the sight of blood, you may need to consider other career options.

SOCIAL WORK AND SOCIAL CARE

Social work is full of uniquely rewarding jobs. If you feel it may be your role in life to help people encountering a range of mental health issues or physical disabilities, then you might find the right career within social work. This sector requires open-minded individuals who are not quick to judge others but have plenty of patience and good humor. This field also includes social care, where professionals provide specialized personal care by supporting individuals in everyday tasks. Social workers in general must have the ability to get along with and understand other people, but they also need to be able to leave work at the end of the day and not take their professional problems home with them.

TO WORK IN HEALTH AND SOCIAL CARE, YOU WILL NEED

●

"people" skills

●

patience

●

a tactful and understanding temperament

●

strength and resilience

●

an open-minded, non-judgmental approach to your work

A care provider has a reassuring talk with an older person. Those wishing to work in health and social care should have a genuine interest in people.

Working in a Core Health Care Role

Health care workers are generally concerned with the health and well-being of people. There are many familiar core, or key, health care roles, such as doctor, nurse, surgeon, midwife, and paramedic.

MEDICAL DOCTORS

Medical doctors gain experience through working in hospitals. Those who stay in hospital medicine go on to specialize in different fields, such as trauma or anesthesiology. Depending on the medical doctor's special field, the job can vary a lot. For example, family practitioners are family doctors who run a practice or are part of a team of doctors. They perform a vital role in the community—listening to, examining, and communicating with patients. They can then diagnose and treat the patient, or refer individuals for specialized treatment.

Doctors educate people about healthier lifestyles and help them understand how to prevent and deal with problems. Doctors also prescribe medicine to patients. Most doctors use computers every day at work for storing patient records, looking up test results, and keeping up-to-date with the latest research on medical conditions.

TO BECOME A DOCTOR, YOU WILL NEED

●

a degree in medicine

●

good communication skills

●

an interest in the well-being of patients

●

dedication and reliability

●

an interest in science and health care

Many doctors are based in hospitals, where they assess a patient's medical condition.

MAIN TASKS: MEDICAL DOCTOR

●

seeing and assessing patients

●

arranging approriate tests and interpreting the results

●

referring cases for specialized treatment

●

reviewing and assessing patients on an ongoing basis

Doctors often have a heavy workload, but they need to spend enough time with each patient to make the correct diagnosis.

Dilip: Medical Doctor

"I decided to become a doctor when I was about 14. I spent a lot of time with children with disabilities and realized that I was very lucky to be healthy and wanted to help people less fortunate than myself. There are many ways you can help people, but I thought being a doctor was best for me . . . I really enjoyed science and found it fascinating to learn about how the body works.

"I like being able to help when people come in and tell me all the things that are wrong with them. I examine them, arrange tests, and put the pieces of the [puzzle] together to find out what the problem is, then I'm usually able to help them. I find it very satisfying when I can make people better. Most people come into [my office] with ongoing problems that take time to cure, but sometimes people can be very ill and need to be managed quickly and efficiently. It is important to be prepared for anything when you come into work each day.

"The job can be difficult at times. It can be very hard when you have to tell people bad news, or if they come in very upset about their lives. Sometimes it is difficult to find the right words to say to comfort them. But I find my job very satisfying and interesting . . . I am glad I decided to become a doctor."

WORKING AS A NURSE

Nurses (both male and female) care for patients, provide support for patients' families and caregivers, and give advice on health and well-being. They need to be excellent communicators, as they work so closely with patients, and they form a crucial part of the health care team, which also includes doctors and physical therapists. Nursing incorporates a wide range of jobs, and nurses can train to specialize within any number of areas: adult care, pediactric care, or mental health care, to name a few. Nurses either work in hospitals or in the community, where patients can receive nursing care and support from public health nurses or home health care nurses, for example. There are nurses working in schools and occupational health nurses working in businesses.

MAIN TASKS: PUBLIC HEALTH NURSE

- *visiting patients at their home*
- *assessing and cleaning patients' wounds*
- *providing patient documentation*
- *working with other team members*
- *promoting healthy living and diet*
- *referring patients to other health care specialists, if required*

HANDY HINT

There are three ways to become a nurse. The major educational paths to becoming a registered nurse (RN) are a bachelor's degree, an associate degree or a diploma from an approved nursing program. RNs with an associate degree or a diploma often later enter bachelor's programs to prepare for a broader scope of nursing practice. RNs may also earn a master's degree, which can lead to more job opportunites.

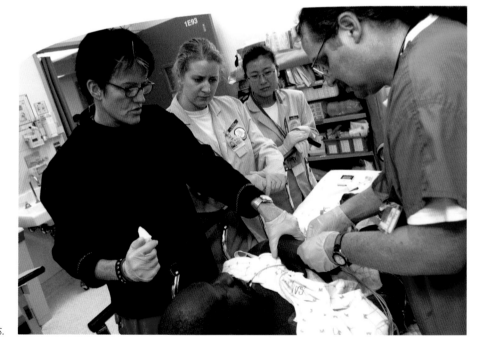

Nurses carefully assess a man's injuries in the emergency room of a hospital. Student nurses learn quickly by witnessing first-hand real-life cases.

Michelle: Public Health Nurse

"At school, I always wanted to be a nurse. My dad was a nurse in the Navy, and I used to love listening to all his stories about the job. I wanted to find out more about people, and working with patients seemed such a good way to do it. So in school, I studied nursing. I also worked as a staff nurse in a hospice for a few years. I enjoyed that, but the great thing about doing nursing is that so many options are open to you.

"I definitely made the right decision to change direction slightly and become a [public health] nurse. I love it. While I was training, I had placements in the community with the [public health program], and it felt like I was learning more with a mentor, on a one-on-one basis. It seemed like such a lovely way to work, thinking on your feet all the time.

"Staff shortages can make the job more difficult, but you still always try to deliver the same level of care to the patients. You have to use communication skills, use assessment skills, and know how to prioritize. You can knock on someone's door and not quite know what's going to happen next. Also, when you enter someone's house, they're more themselves, so that can be more of a challenge sometimes! But I love the patients, even when they're difficult. The patients make the job what it is —this is the only job I want to do."

Home health care nurses spend a large part of their time visiting patients in their homes or in residential care facilities.

WORKING AS A MIDWIFE

Midwives care for mothers and their babies during labor and birth. Most births take place in a hospital, although a growing number of mothers give birth at home. Midwives can opt to work with hospital or home births. They assist women throughout the birthing process in low-risk cases, only calling a doctor if there are complications. Midwives also help mothers and babies during pregnancy and in the early days of the newborn baby's life.

HELP IS AT HAND

Midwives provide prenatal care for expectant mothers and may also run childbirth classes for pregnant women and their partners. After the birth, a midwife offers follow-up care and is able to offer a range of counseling skills. New mothers may sometimes find breastfeeding difficult, or they may suffer from postpartum depression; some expectant mothers may miscarry. A midwife is there to support women through difficult times.

MAIN TASKS:
MIDWIFE

● *providing prenatal care*

● *carrying out follow-up care*

● *assisting with births*

● *helping mothers feel in control*

● *working with other team members*

● *providing childbirth classes*

HANDY HINT

If you are male and think you would like to become a midwife, you will be in a minority, but it is certainly possible. You will need to be calm, reassuring, and able to empathize. As long as you have the correct training to look after mother and baby, you can pursue a career in midwifery. You will also need to be sensitive to the fact that some mothers, because of their religion, culture, or simply personal choice, will prefer to have a woman as a midwife.

Most midwives are women, but men can also become midwives. They help teach the skills needed by new mothers to breastfeed, change diapers, and bathe their babies.

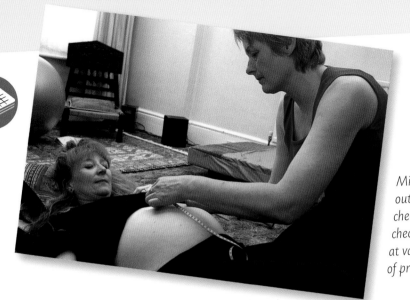

Midwives carry out prenatal checkups, checking growth at various stages of pregnancy.

Anne: Midwife

"My [mother] was a nurse, and I always wanted to be one, too. First I did general nursing, which included two months of midwifery. Working with women appealed to me, and initially midwifery was something I thought I'd like to do. Once I'd started the training, I knew it was for me.

"You're in a very privileged position as a midwife. You're invited into people's homes, and you get to know the [mother-to-be], the family, the children . . . You see them through such a special time—most women only do this once or twice in their lives. I'd probably do the job without pay . . . no, I wouldn't be able to afford to, but that's the way you feel. It's a job you never tire of.

"It can be very upsetting if a pregnant woman loses a baby, but we provide support for [mothers], so they can talk things through with us. Often you've already built up quite a relationship with them. You need to have a caring nature in this job.

"With home births, you're on call, so you must be available to go. When the call comes in, your heart starts going. But when you're at the birth, you have to be calm . . . and you have to be patient. Home births are low risk, and things are more relaxed at home."

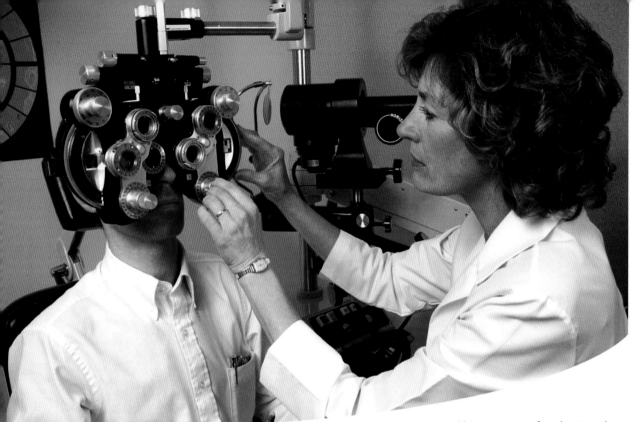

THE EYES HAVE IT

Another important specialized field in health care is concerned with vision and is known as optometry. There is a range of jobs with quite similar-sounding names: optometrist, opthamologist, and dispensing optician. Optometrists examine eyes, measuring defective vision and determining lens prescriptions. Opthamologists perform eye surgery as well as diagnose and treat eye diseases and injuries. Dispensing opticians do not conduct eye examinations but fill eye prescriptions. All professions require good communication skills and a strong interest in science.

Using a range of sophisticated instruments, an optometrist carries out an eye examination. A patient may require glasses to correct an abnormality.

DENTISTRY

Dentistry is an important sector of health care specializing in not only the teeth, but also the mouth and gums. Dentists diagnose problems of the mouth and aim to prevent tooth decay and gum disease. They examine and clean patients' teeth and gums, as well as filling, crowning, repairing, and extracting teeth where necessary. Teamwork is important because while most dentists work alone in their own practice, they are part of a team of professionals such as dental assistants, technicians, and hygienists.

HANDY HINT
If you want to become a dentist, you will need eight years of education beyond high school. Find a university with a dental school attached—you will study anatomy, physiology, and pathology as well as practical aspects of dentistry. To become licensed, you will have to pass National Board Dental Examinations.

Jennifer: Dental Assistant

"I started the job as a dental [assistant] working just one day a week within a private practice. Then the opportunity came to work at another location, training on the job while going to college.

"I like the change of tempo at work. There are times when I'm very busy assisting the dentist with patients, and others when I work alone and [keep busy] with jobs that keep the practice up-to-date. My day is always varied—the unexpected can happen, and it is essential to work in a flexible manner. Each day's appointment list is usually pretty full, but there may suddenly be an emergency . . . and you need to book that in as well, so you may be stretched sometimes. The hours can be long, and you need good health yourself to function well.

"I work closely with the dentist, so it's important to build a good rapport and a way of working that is good for both of you. As a dental assistant, you have to think about the needs of the dentist and the patient, as well as the parent, if the patient is a child."

A dental assistant will work closely with the dentist during procedures, making sure that all the instruments are properly sterilized and ready to use.

**MAIN TASKS:
DENTAL ASSISTANT**

●

assisting the dentist in procedures

●

making sure the patient is comfortable

●

assisting with processing x-ray films

●

educating patients on dental care

FINDING A JOB
PARAMEDIC

Paramedics may be employed by fire departments, hospitals, or private ambulance services. A high school diploma is required to enter an emergency medical technician training program. Training is offered at progressive levels—EMT-Basic, EMT-Intermediate, and EMT-Paramedic—and students learn skills ranging from basic emergency care to advanced medical skills.

Paramedics respond to medical emergencies and are first on the scene at car accidents. They start any necessary treatment.

FROM SUPPORT STAFF TO SURGEONS

There are many other vital health care professions. Some, such as a paramedic or ambulance driver, are very visible roles. Others may be more behind the scenes, such as an administrator or lab technician. But all health care workers play a vital part in the smooth and efficient running of a hospital or health practice. Support workers may move equipment and supplies and ensure that patients are transported to the correct room. Surgical technologists make sure that all hospital instruments, such as needles and scalpels and other equipment, are meticulously clean and safe to use. Surgeons carry out operations on patients with injuries and diseases, or to improve the quality of life for people with conditions that are gradually worsening.

A huge range of health care roles exist. If you are a good communicator, work well in a team, have plenty of initiative, and are genuinely interested in the welfare of patients, you are likely to find an exciting profession that matches your attributes.

EMERGENCY!

Ambulance staff include ambulance drivers, emergency medical technicians (EMTs), and paramedics. Drivers can respond fast to an emergency call, arriving at the scene of an accident or at someone's home. Paramedics and EMTs will examine the patient on site, for example, following a car accident, or after a suspected

heart attack. They will then take action, giving the patient immediate, appropriate care and transferring the person to a hospital as quickly and as safely as possible. Individuals looking for a career in this field will need to be calm under pressure, be able to think on their feet, and make the right decisions.

SMOOTH RUNNING

Receptionists answer telephone calls, make appointments, and are there to meet and greet visitors to clinics and hospitals, while health administrators can work within different departments to assist with the running of the offices. Hospitals and other health care practices need well-maintained health records so that key medical staff can consult files and computer databases and quickly retrieve up-to-date patient information. Health records staff provide this vital service.

Using considerable leadership and communication skills, health service managers are responsible for the smooth running of various health services, ensuring that they are delivered efficiently. Clinic managers run doctor's offices, financial managers manage budgets, and information systems managers use IT (information technology) to monitor performance and improve patient care in a hospital, for example. Skillful and experienced managers can become directors and chief executives.

Mental health service workers assist in administrative duties at a psychiatric center. They work together in a team.

WHERE WILL I BE?
As a doctor, you may choose to specialize in a field such as obstetrics/gynecology, orthopedics, dermatology, family practice, surgery or many others.

Other Health Care Jobs

Alongside the core health care professions, there are a lot of other jobs concerned with taking care of people's physical and mental well-being. If a doctor thinks a patient needs it, he or she may refer that patient to one of a range of specialists who can help.

COUNSELING

Not all health problems are physical; many are caused by mental health issues. People sometimes need help coping with a difficult short-term problem, such as the loss of a job, or with a longer-term condition, such as depression. Mental health professionals include counselors, psychotherapists, psychologists, and psychiatrists. These terms sometimes cause confusion, as the roles can overlap. Counselors help people talk about their feelings and behavior confidentially in a quiet, safe setting. By listening carefully and asking questions, counselors are able to help people find solutions to their personal problems. In this way, counselors can help a client handle his or her everyday life better.

TO BECOME A COUNSELOR, YOU WILL NEED
•
listening and observational skills
•
patience and sensitivity
•
an ability to build trust

HANDY HINT
Education requirements for counselors vary based on area of specialty and state licensing requirements. A master's degree is usually required to be licensed as a counselor, but some states accept a bachelor's degree with appropriate counseling courses. Some employers provide training for newly hired counselors. Others may offer time off or tuition assistance to complete a graduate degree. Often, counselors must participate in continuing education to maintain their certificates and licenses.

People suffering from a particular problem, such as alcoholism or grief after a close relative's death, often find it useful to take part in group therapy.

A counselor will encourage a client to talk about her own feelings and listen very carefully.

Caroline: Counselor

"I was 16 when I left school, and I felt lost about what my future would hold. At such a young age, it can be so difficult to know what direction to take. Later, when I was studying for my bachelor's degree, I met a tutor who inspired me and changed my life. She was trained as a counselor, and when I was in her class, I felt completely connected to what she was teaching. All of a sudden, I felt like I understood what I wanted to do with my life.

"As a counselor, you create an honest and respectful relationship with your client. It is a privilege for someone to share his or her deepest feelings with you. Counseling is a difficult job because you have to work at the client's pace and not be judgmental about what you hear. Sometimes a client shares something that reminds you of a personal issue you have not resolved yourself—and that is when you need to look at your personal response within your own counseling."

Music therapists can work in a variety of settings, including hospices for the terminally ill. Hospices help families by making the end of patients' lives more enjoyable.

ALL SORTS OF THERAPY

A wide variety of therapists work within the health care sector. An art therapist can help someone with learning disabilities express his or her feelings through art. A speech and language therapist can help patients with communication problems and eating, drinking, and swallowing disorders. A music therapist can use music and sound to help someone with mental health problems or behavioral difficulties. These therapists work very closely with other professionals, including nurses, physical therapists, psychologists, social workers, and teachers, as well as occupational therapists.

GAINING CONFIDENCE

An occupational therapist's job involves the kinds of things that occupy people every day, including looking after themselves, working, and relaxing. Occupational therapists help people with physical, mental, or social problems to gain more control and confidence. Along with other members of the health and social care team, occupational therapists enable their clients to make the most of their abilities so that they live as complete a life as possible.

FINDING SMART SOLUTIONS

If, for example, an older woman with arthritis is struggling to fill a kettle for a cup of tea, an occupational therapist can work out a solution. This might involve installing special equipment in the woman's home or adapting the client's kitchen to suit her needs. The therapist would devise a different plan of action for different situations, for example, if a person is suffering from Alzheimer's disease. Occupational therapists can work in hospitals, hospices, residential homes, clinics, schools, colleges, or prisons to look after the needs of a wide range of clients. Part-time and flexible work, as well as private practice, is also possible.

TO BECOME AN OCCUPATIONAL THERAPIST, YOU WILL NEED

●

a genuine interest in people

●

a caring nature

●

adaptability and resourcefulness

Alice: Occupational Therapist

"What I enjoy about being an occupational therapist is also what can often make my job a difficult and demanding one, but it is never boring or repetitive! Every person I work with has his or her own difficulties—from the young child who [walks with a limp] and finds school life difficult to the elderly adult who relies on a wheelchair to get around and needs advice to redesign her kitchen. My job is to assist and enable individuals to achieve their maximum level of independence and functioning. This is challenging, as every one of us has different ideas, goals, family support, and living environments that affect what we want to achieve in life. For a person with a disability, what we would consider minor actions, such as putting on socks and shoes, can be a major achievement.

"One of the attractions of the job is the different individuals we work with, plus the variety of working environments, such as hospitals, schools, people's own homes, and workplaces. When people disregard your advice or have no desire to achieve agreed goals, the job can be frustrating. But what's great about it is that there is huge scope for job satisfaction."

An occupational therapist can assess a patient's movement skills using a peg board.

PHARMACISTS

Pharmacists are experts on the use of medicine. Hospital pharmacists' work includes dispensing medicine to patients and managing the hospital's pharmacy services. Many pharmacists work in community pharmacies, from health care centers to independent drugstores and large chain pharmacies; they prepare certain medicines and dispense drugs to members of the public. Other pharmacists work for private companies in the pharmaceutical industry. All pharmacists need to be good at science and be accurate, methodical, and responsible.

FINDING A JOB
PHARMACIST

Pharmacists must earn a Pharm.D. degree from an accredited college or school of pharmacy. To be admitted to a Pharm.D. program, an applicant must have completed at least two years of postsecondary study. Other entry requirements usually include math and science courses, in subjects such as chemistry, biology, and physics. Students in Pharm.D. programs also spend about one-fourth of their time in supervised pharmacy practice settings. In order to obtain a license to practice, a pharmacy student must also pass a series of exams.

RADIOLOGIC TECHNOLOGIST

Radiologic technologists work mainly in hospital imaging departments, emergency rooms, and operating rooms, using x-rays, ultrasound, and other sophisticated equipment to produce images of human organs and limbs. A patient with a fractured wrist visiting the emergency room in a hospital would be seen by a radiologic technologist, who would take an x-ray to aid diagnosis and treatment.

PHYSICAL THERAPISTS

Physical therapists treat patients suffering from a wide range of injuries, illnesses, and conditions. They massage and manipulate soft tissue, and they recommend exercises to improve a patient's mobility. Most physical therapists work in hospitals, clinics, or private offices, and some visit patients in their own homes.

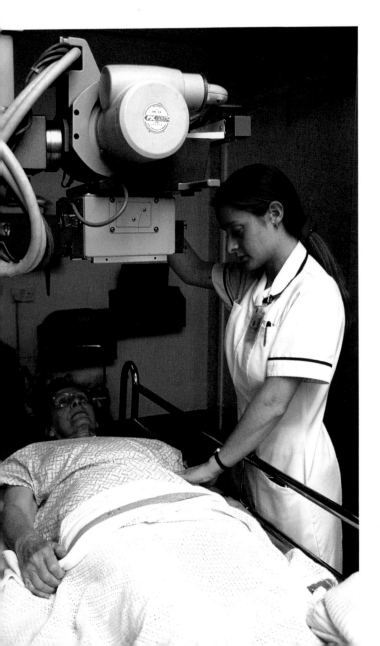

A radiologic technologist will assess a patient's needs before using imaging equipment. An x-ray will help diagnose the problem.

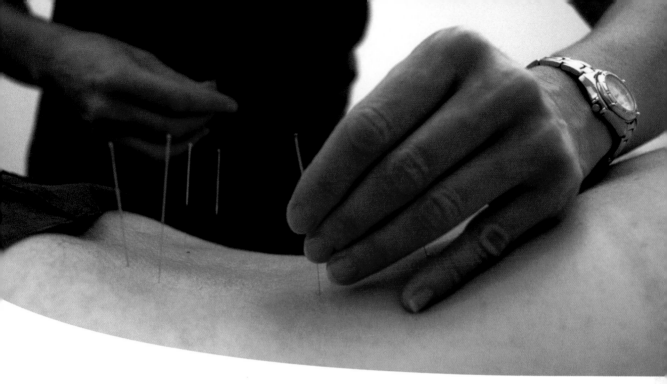

COMPLEMENTARY MEDICINE

There are careers within health care that do not fit neatly into the traditional framework of medicine as we know it. This is often referred to as "complementary medicine." Many patients find complementary medicine a useful alternative, and some alternative treatments are now used alongside more traditional methods. Complementary medicine practitioners include osteopaths, chiropractors, acupuncturists, massage therapists, reflexologists, and homeopaths.

An osteopath uses a holistic approach to the human body and tries to relieve pain and correct abnormalities using manipulation. Patients may be referred to osteopaths by traditional physicans, but usually they visit an osteopath as the result of personal recommendation. Chiropractors treat problems with joints, bones, and muscles and use their hands on the body's joints—in particular, the spine—to make focused adjustments to improve function. Acupuncturists use an ancient form of Chinese medicine to heal. They examine patients carefully and find out their medical history before inserting needles into the skin to stimulate key points and regulate the entire body.

Like traditional health workers, complementary therapists need to have good communication skills and should inspire trust in their patients and other health care professionals. They also need manual dexterity. For certain disciplines, such as osteopathy, training can take as long as five years. Once qualified, most complementary therapists become self-employed.

An acupuncturist inserts fine needles into a patient's skin. Acupuncturists use a holistic approach to healing and treat imbalances in the body.

WHERE WILL I BE?
While many practitioners of complementary medicine are self-employed or work in centers that specialize in that type of therapy, many are now being hired in traditional hospitals and clinics. More and more, tradional medicine is seeing the value in complementary medicine.

Social Work

Social workers support vulnerable groups in society, such as children and families, people with physical disabilities, and those with mental health problems. They assess people's needs and to try to find lasting solutions to problems they may have.

MAIN TASKS: SOCIAL WORKER

- *assessing situations and individuals' needs*
- *organizing support*
- *developing relationships with individuals and families*
- *working with other professionals*
- *writing reports and keeping records*
- *attending court hearings*

WORK INVOLVING CHILDREN

Social workers tend to specialize within a particular field, for example, in the care and protection of children. Work of this type can be stressful, as children may have been abused by their parents or caregivers, physically, emotionally, or sexually. Social workers visit children and their families in the home, or they may escort children on visits to their parents or families if they are being looked after elsewhere. A social worker may have to make the decision that an abused child should be removed from his or her parents. In this case, the social worker then has to help find a new home for the child.

HANDY HINT
It's important to be able to empathize with the problems of children and families. As social work can be very stressful, one of the most important qualities in a social worker is the ability to leave the job behind and "switch off" at the end of the day.

A social worker has to develop trust quickly with people. Workers may use props like dolls to help determine if a child has suffered abuse.

A social worker interviews a father and his children at home. Social workers must handle pressure, as they will have difficult situations to face.

Scott: Social Worker (Child Protection)

"The thing I enjoy most about my job is the sheer variety. You never know what challenges you will have to deal with when you first arrive at the office. They could range from carrying out a joint interview with the police, doing an assessment for a child with disabilities, or supervising contact with a parent and her or his children. A significant amount of my job is child protection. I spend two to three days a week on duty, and this involves taking calls from both the public and professionals. This can be daunting sometimes, as often we have little information on families, and our assessments need to be as thorough as possible to ensure the best outcome for the child. Working together with police, health [care providers], and [educators] is another key element of social work. You definitely need to have good listening skills and the ability to stick with people when the going gets tough.

"If we don't have enough resources, we can't always provide proper service for clients. This can obviously be frustrating for both worker and service user. Doing all the paperwork is time consuming, but it's important to keep up-to-date records. When the job gets really difficult, I find a good sense of humor helps."

FOSTERING AND ADOPTION

Social workers in the fostering and adoption sector assess whether couples or families are going to make suitable caregivers for children who have lost their parents or been removed from their care. Social workers can help find short- or long-term solutions for children with a foster family, or in a permanent home with people who are willing to adopt. Social workers can also provide support for families who agree to foster or adopt a child.

MENTAL HEALTH WORKERS

Social workers who specialize in the mental health sector work with people with a range of mental health needs. For example, a social worker may be assigned to an older person with memory problems following the onset of Alzheimer's disease or a young adult suffering from depression or schizophrenia. Mental health workers assess their clients' different needs and try to help them adapt and cope with everyday life. They may visit clients every day to help make meals and check medication. Social workers have the power to remove people from their homes if they are likely to be a danger to themselves or others in their family or the community.

Mental health workers work as a team to look after a man in a nursing home. Workers need to have a compassionate nature to help people.

TO BECOME A MENTAL HEALTH WORKER, YOU WILL NEED

●

a real interest in people's welfare

●

excellent communication skills

●

the ability to handle pressure

HANDY HINT

If you are interested in working in the mental health sector, study subjects such as social work, psychology, and sociology in college.

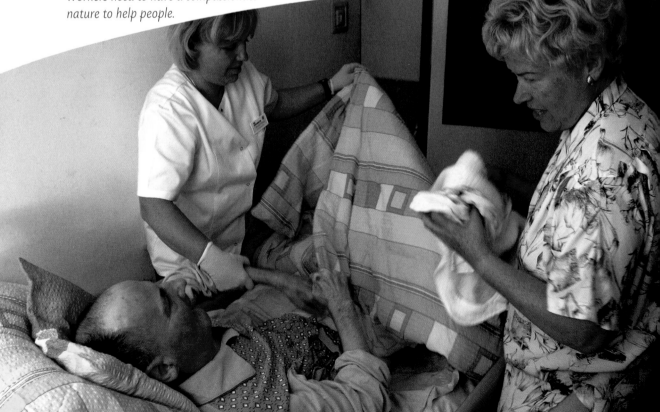

A mental health worker can help a client learn new skills, such as how to use a computer.

Tyler: Mental Health Worker

"I work with people who have all sorts of different mental health needs. When I go into someone's home, I assess what type of help they need. We then try to support them and give them a chance to live independently in their own homes.

"I studied to become a social worker and quickly realized that I wanted to specialize in mental health care. My grandfather had Alzheimer's for many years, and I think that experience made me want to help other people cope with mental health disorders. I'm outgoing and enjoy working with different people. As well as clients, I also work with psychiatric nurses and psychiatrists, monitoring and reviewing people with mental health problems. Friends have told me I'm good at problem solving—I think this helps in the job, too. It's important not to judge people, as well.

"There can be plenty of paperwork and updating of records on the computer. I much prefer the hands-on time I have working with clients, but I have to balance this with time in the office. You also have to keep up to speed with any developments in mental health—[new information and methods are constantly being introduced]. Social work is hard, but I find it rewarding, as you can make a difference in someone's life."

Probation officers need to be able to present information. A probation officer gives a lecture on the dangers of reckless driving to young offenders.

YOUTH AND COMMUNITY WORKERS

Youth and community workers help young people to grow, learn, and develop as individuals, and they encourage them to play a positive role in their community. They might work in a school, youth club, community center, church, or mosque. Here, they help young people organize projects or activities, such as service work in their community.

CRIMINAL JUSTICE SERVICES

Other community workers are employed within the criminal justice services sector. Social workers in this field include parole officers and probation officers. Although their roles are different, both work to protect the public and promote community safety.

Parole officers' work of crime prevention and promotion of safety within the community involves working with offenders and prisoners during and after their sentences. The parole officer will prepare a report when an offender attends court, looking at family and education. The officer meets the offender and his or her family and identifies the individual's needs and the risks. The parole officer works out a plan to help prevent the person from reoffending and continues to assess the offender and his or her potential risk to the public.

FINDING A JOB
If you'd like to become a social worker, a good way to gain vital experience is to do volunteer work in a social care or community setting. If you like the work, you can then train to be a social worker. A four-year degree in social work will combine study with plenty of practical experience. Decide which sector of social work you are most likely to enjoy. Are you more suited to working with children and families, the elderly, people with mental health problems, or those with physical disabilities? Or maybe you prefer to work with offenders? Once you have completed your training in social work, there should be plenty of job opportunities.

TO BECOME A PROBATION OR PAROLE OFFICER, YOU WILL NEED

●

the ability to work in a team

●

patience and firmness

●

a genuine interest in helping people

●

an understanding of criminal law

Probation officers may decide to recommend a team-building course as part of a rehabilitation program for young offenders.

ONE-ON-ONE

Probation officers supervise low-risk offenders who have been placed on probation rather than sent to prison. Their job is to support offenders serving community and custodial sentences. To help change offenders' behavior, they will oversee rehabilitation programs for people in custody and after release. They may also provide a supporting role to victims of crime and their families.

Both probation and parole officers supervise offenders through personal contact. They also manage offenders sentenced with a community or court order, making sure that offenders follow orders of the court, such as unpaid work for the community. It can be a difficult job building a one-on-one relationship with an offender, as these officers will need to try to strike a balance between firmness and helping the offender to develop self-respect.

MAIN TASKS
SUBSTANCE ABUSE COUNSELOR

- *assessing new referrals*
- *developing and implementing care plans with clients*
- *developing trust with clients*
- *providing ongoing evaluation of clients' needs*
- *working with other agencies*
- *maintaining accurate records*

REHABILITATION

Social workers in rehabilitation try to help restore a person's skills and make the most of their abilities. Rehabilitation programs exist to help a variety of people. Criminal offenders may need rehabilitation to assist their return into the community, while people with hearing impairment or partial sight may need help developing their abilities to cope with everyday life.

DRUG AND ALCOHOL PROBLEMS

Social workers may specialize in rehabilitation for individuals with substance abuse problems, or addiction to drugs or alcohol. For example, substance abuse counselors can help clients who have recently entered treatment for drug or alcohol abuse. Substance abuse counselors will help draw up a treatment plan for people who are in the process of addressing their problem, and will help to provide one-on-one, group, and professional support. They often work together with other professionals in health care, social care, and criminal justice teams. They have to work hard to win substance abusers' trust, and they give constructive support, education, and guidance.

Substance abuse counselors can provide education and one-on-one counseling to young people who have become dependent on alcohol.

WHERE WILL I BE?
From social worker, you can progress to supervisory roles. Alternatively, you might decide to opt for self-employment as a counselor or therapist.

Vinnie Marino, a former drug addict, teaches a yoga class. Channeling energy in a creative way can help addicts to recover.

Caroline: Substance Abuse Counselor

"I just love the diversity of the job—no two days are the same. I find working with people a challenge and enjoy helping them to learn more about themselves and how they can change their lives by looking at the choices they make. You need to be able to listen, but sometimes it's also important in this job to challenge their views respectfully. Sometimes the level of nonattendance of the client group we work with is frustrating, even though I am aware that this seems to come with the job. You do need to have patience.

"By far, the most challenging aspect of the job is ensuring that goals set for the client are his or her own goals, and not influenced by [counselors'] own values or beliefs.

"My previous jobs have been as a psychiatric nurse. I have always been intrigued by how people behave and interact. I became interested in the field of addiction while working in psychiatric wards. I like the idea that everyone has the ability to change for the better with the right support. I don't hold the view that being addicted to a substance means an individual has failed. It only means they've made the wrong choices . . . and those choices can be reversed."

Direct Care

Workers in direct care provide hands-on, quality personal care and support for people with various practical, social, and emotional needs. They work in many different settings, including nursing homes and children's residential units. They also work in people's own homes to help them maintain their independence.

RESIDENTIAL CARE

Residential care aides provide vital hands-on care in residential homes or secure institutions for people in need of 24-hour care on a long-term or temporary basis. They may help children or young adults with physical disabilities or mental health problems, or provide assistance to older people unable to continue living in their own home. Work varies greatly depending on the setting and the people cared for. Sometimes residential care aides will help people carry out practical, day-to-day tasks such as getting dressed. At other times they may give encouragement and support, or sit and listen carefully to a person's problems. Residential care aides do not necessarily need to live in the home themselves; some go there to work and leave at the end of the working day. Residential care aides are supervised by residential care managers.

TO BE A RESIDENTIAL CARE AIDE, YOU WILL NEED
●
good communication skills
●
a positive outlook
●
patience and empathy
●
a genuine desire to provide care

A residential care aide tries to make sure that each resident is as comfortable and happy as possible.

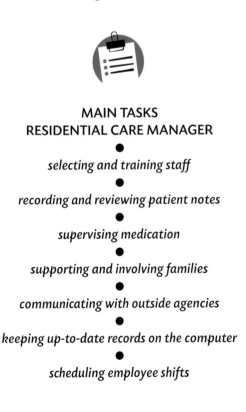

MAIN TASKS
RESIDENTIAL CARE MANAGER
●
selecting and training staff
●
recording and reviewing patient notes
●
supervising medication
●
supporting and involving families
●
communicating with outside agencies
●
keeping up-to-date records on the computer
●
scheduling employee shifts

A member of staff in a care facility reads with a resident who suffers from dementia.

David: Residential Care Manager

"Having had plenty of nursing and care experience with older people, I now hold a position of great responsibility as a residential care manager, maintaining the standards of care for 35 residents and the welfare of very hardworking care staff.

"A difficult part of my job involves dealing with the deaths that occur. We get to know the people in our care and become close to them and their families. We are very much like one large family living in a large house, so usually everyone is affected when someone dies. I look after the families (and staff who may not have experienced death) because they may need lots of support. It may be a very sad time, but it is also a time when we work very closely together to support and care for one another as a team. I try to use it as a learning experience so that we can improve the care for the next person we support.

"Although I work about 60 hours each week, I enjoy every moment, whether I am providing medication, dealing with wounds, carrying out reviews in the hospital, or listening to our residents telling me about their life. It is the challenge of ensuring that those who have chosen to spend their remaining years at the nursing home receive the best treatment possible that makes my job worthwhile."

CARE AT HOME

Home care aides provide special assistance to older clients or people with physical disabilities in their own homes. Depending on the clients' needs, home care aides visit their homes up to three or four times a day, making sure that they feed themselves properly and helping with other tasks around the home. The work is likely to involve household chores, such as cleaning, emptying the trash, and making beds. Home care aides may also help clients take a bath, or they may supervise their medication. The aide's role is to try to ensure that people can live as independently as possible in their own home.

ORGANIZING HOME CARE

Case managers assess an individual's needs as well as his or her financial circumstances. They assess whether someone is eligible for support or not, then help to arrange home care to cover specific needs. Case managers provide training and give support to aides. Most people working in the field of home care are employed by local government or by private care agencies.

MAIN TASKS
HOME CARE AIDE

●

providing assistance and care for clients

●

helping with bathing or showering

●

making meals or preparing food

●

carrying out other household tasks

●

listening to clients

●

carrying out first aid, if necessary

TO BE A HOME CARE AIDE,
YOU WILL NEED

●

patience and a calm approach

●

generosity of spirit

●

sensitivity

A home care aide will need to be able to empathize with people who may become upset or frustrated. She will also help with day-to-day practicalities.

Home care aides provide a great service for many older people. Their support helps those who like their independence.

Berenice: Home Care Aide

"I love that I can make just a little difference to people's lives. You don't need to have worked in care before, but I think you must have a heart. Sometimes laughter is what people want to hear—it's no use [being down] as this will only depress people . . . and that's not what this job is about.

"With caring, you do become attached to people, especially when you work with them two or three times a day. It can be a bit of a roller coaster at times, especially with clients with mental issues, as they have their good and bad days. You have to look at the person, not their disability. When your clients get ill or pass away, it can be very emotional, as you do bond with them, and you grieve.

"It's great to encourage clients to do things about the house, like making a cup of coffee, baking a cake, or planting some bulbs in the garden. All these things keep them physically active . . . and it helps to keep their mind active, too. I go shopping with some, which gives them a great boost, as they don't have to rely on their families for help. We give so little but get so much back. It's a very rewarding job."

Adult day care providers help with duties such as serving coffee to older people at a drop-in center. Care providers look after the welfare of the people and provide company.

ADULT DAY CARE

Direct care jobs also involve looking after older people at day care centers. People tend to arrive at the centers during the morning, then they have lunch and leave during the afternoon. Day care providers help people with practical daily activities, such as eating or going to the bathroom. They also organize social activities such as games and trips.

Day care providers need to be able to get along well with people from many different backgrounds. They also need a flexible approach to their work, so that they can cope when sudden changes are necessary or if there's an emergency. A trip out from the center can be fun for members, but it needs to be very well organized, with the right amount of staff and alternative plans in case things do not run as smoothly as expected.

FINDING A JOB

Job prospects in the home care field are excellent due to a rise in the number of elderly people, who welcome home care as an alternative to an expensive nursing home or hospital care. Find opportunities through local government health offices, elder care programs, and home health care agencies. While some states require formal training (usually offered through community or technical colleges), in others, on-the-job training is all that is required.

SOUNDING THE ALARM

If you are a person who cares about the welfare of others, a job in social and emergency assistance may be for you. Employees in these occupations run programs to fill people's basic needs, such as food or housing. Or, when disaster strikes, they offer emergency shelter and necessities. Vocational rehabilitation service employees teach life skills to disabled people, so they can live as independently as possible.

Employees in this field will work with a wide variety of people. A community housing service program, for example, may work with women seeking emergency shelter for themselves and their children after escaping domestic abuse. Or, it may be involved in planning and building houses through an organization such as Habitat for Humanity.

HANDY HINT
If you think you have the right personal qualities to be a home care aide, see if you can shadow one in his or her job. This will help you get an idea of the type of work involved.

WHERE WILL I BE?
If you are interested in a career in home care, one of the routes you might follow is first to become a home care aide. From here, you could progress to become a case manager or take more classes to become a home health nurse.

Residential care facilities are a good option for some older people. Residential home assistants help the residents.

Child and Youth Services

Child care is an increasingly important service, as most parents go to work. Child care provision includes professionals in home or institutional day care centers and early education settings, such as preschools.

CHILD CARE PROVIDERS

Child care providers are involved in early education. Their jobs vary according to their setting and responsibilities. For example, a preschool teacher usually provides care and education to children between the ages of three and five. Child care workers generally look after children from birth to about seven years of age. They plan and organize a wide variety of early learning activities to develop children's social, emotional, physical, and creative abilities. By involving children as individuals and in groups, child care providers encourage learning through play, practical skills, and reading. They also promote good behavior and make sure children are safe in their care. Child care providers may also work in private family homes as nannies.

TO BECOME A CHILD CARE PROVIDER, YOU WILL NEED

● *a love of children*

● *creativity and imagination*

● *excellent communication and listening skills*

● *the ability to work as part of a team*

MAIN TASKS PRESCHOOL TEACHER

● *planning individual and group activities*

● *supporting young children in their learning through play and activities*

● *creating opportunities for role play, games, singing, and more*

● *encouraging confidence and independence of children*

● *ensuring children's safety*

● *promoting positive behavior*

Child care providers can help young children to develop and learn in a happy and safe environment.

Preschool teachers also work with smaller numbers of children whenever possible to establish closer bonds.

May: Preschool Teacher

"I love the variety and flexibility of the job, combining child-centered and adult-planned activities and supporting a child's learning through play. I have different groups in the morning and the afternoon, with girls and boys of three to five, at all stages of development. Each group has up to 10 children, and each child is assigned a key worker. This enables the worker to get to know the child individually and build a relationship with the child and his or her parents.

"The job is physically and mentally demanding and involves daily planning, keeping written records of observations and photos for each child, and always ensuring that the child has resources to extend and challenge his or her learning through play. I love to see the children develop. They start nursery life as little extensions of their moms and dads, and by the time they leave to go to [kindergarten], they're more confident and independent individuals. It's fascinating to watch a child's development. They learn the most in their first five years. Our activities [in the preschool] are challenging—it's like planting a seed and watching it develop. I have a real pride in the children, and I try to treat them as I would my own. I find the job very rewarding and satisfying."

ACTIVITY COORDINATORS

An activity coordinator's job involves planning and supervising play opportunities for children and young people in their leisure time. Activity coordinators usually work before or after school, on weekends, and during school holidays, so most of the jobs tend to be part time or seasonal. Activity coordinators give children the chance to experiment through play, either in or out of the usual school setting. Other locations for activities might be youth clubs, leisure or community centers, churches, and community park and recreation programs.

The demand for activity coordinators is likely to continue in the future, as an increasing number of parents look for flexible child care options while they work. Employers include local authorities, volunteer and charitable organizations, and children's party planners.

FINDING A JOB

If you are interested in becoming an activity coordinator, try to gain some experience in working with children, especially in larger groups. Offer babysitting services to friends and family and contact volunteer and charitable organizations, park and rec departments, and children's party planners for possible openings. Research jobs through local papers and on the Internet.

Activity coordinators try to encourage children to take risks in a safe environment, such as an adventure playground.

MAIN TASKS
ACTIVITY COORDINATOR

●

organizing groups of children for games

●

preparing craft activities

●

supervising children at all times

●

providing children with a safe environment

●

monitoring and evaluating play sessions and events

●

encouraging children to experiment through play

●

promoting good behavior in children

Activity coordinators can have fun enjoying activities such as the parachute game. This sort of activity includes everyone.

Katrina: Activity Coordinator

"After leaving school I did four years of fairly meaningless work, then I [worked as a nanny] which made me realize I wanted to work with children. I started to look for a job with children locally. I found a job working in a day care center and started my child care training. I'd been working in this sort of environment for about two years, but I began to find it a bit restrictive and [wanted] something different. Around the same time, an opportunity became available to volunteer as an activity coordinator for a local charity. I enjoyed it so much that when a paid position came up, I applied [right] away. I got the job and have been working as an activity coordinator ever since.

"As I run open-access play sessions, I never know how well attended they will be, which makes it hard to prepare for, but this adds to the variety of the job. It's harder when young people show challenging behavior, as this can spoil other children's enjoyment. But I really like working with a wide range of age groups in my job, outdoors, and in all sorts of locations. I also enjoy playing and being creative with the children I work with."

SCHOOL SOCIAL WORKERS

Many children and young people have serious problems at home, which can affect their lives and the lives of other students and teachers at school. Some children get bullied within the school itself. School social workers and psychologists have important roles, within a varied team of professionals, to focus on the happiness and well-being of students.

School social workers work with educators to help resolve problems with particular students. If a child or young person is not attending school regularly, a school social worker can act as a link to discuss concerns among the school, the student, and the parents or caregivers. School social workers also work closely with health professionals, educational psychologists, teachers, and police officers. They address issues that arise, for example, when children and young people are frequently absent or at risk of suspension from school. They try to get to the bottom of the problem and help the student return to school.

WHERE WILL I BE?

If you are interested in a career working with young children, think about training to become a preschool teacher. With experience, you could then rise to the position of assistant director and eventually director of the school. Alternatively, you could look into running your own private day care center.

MAIN TASKS SCHOOL SOCIAL WORKER

●

assessing problems and working on solutions

●

sharing information with fellow professionals

●

trying to improve links between school and home

●

supporting suspended students on return to school

●

writing reports on cases

●

giving evidence in court

School social workers can assess any problems in the home.

A school counselor keeps an open mind as he tries to establish trust with a young person.

Pete: School Counselor

"I like the challenge of making and maintaining relationships with young people to try to support them in resolving their difficulties. We offer lots of advice and support to parents and [caregivers] on managing young people's behavior and in communicating with them. Many of the parents to whom we offer support lack the experience and quite often the will to bring up their children in appropriate ways. I particularly enjoy the challenge of relating to adolescents, whom I feel are the most misunderstood group in society. You have to have a positive regard for others and be able to separate people from their behavior, because these two things can be completely different.

"In any work like this, you have to accept that there are some things you can do very little about. That's hard sometimes, and you tend to carry those issues around with you. Some young people's difficulties are due to poor role modeling by adults, at home as well as in school, and adolescents are often the victims of people judging them. I think we need to build trust and develop our understanding of people with difficulties... only then can we provide proper support to try to resolve difficulties in a real and lasting way. I believe this type of work is more of a vocation than a job—I really couldn't see myself doing anything else."

Further Information

BOOKS

American Medical Association. *Health Care Careers Directory.* American Medical Association, 2009-2010 (updated yearly).

Association of American Medical Colleges Staff. *Medical School Admission Requirements.* Association of American Medical Colleges, 2010-2011 (updated yearly).

DuBois, Brenda and Karla Krogsrud Miley. *Social Work: An Empowering Profession.* Allyn and Bacon, 20011.

Field, Shelly. *Career Opportunities in Health Care.* Ferguson, 2007.

Ritter, Jessica. *101 Careers in Social Work.* Springer Publishing, 2009.

Turner, Susan Odegaard. *Nursing Career Planning Guide.* Jones and Bartlett Publishers, 2007.

WEB SITES

www.bls.gov/oco
For hundreds of different types of jobs in the health care and social work fields, the Occupational Outlook Handbook gives information on education needed, earnings, job prospects, and more.

careers.socialworkers.org
Explore the social work profession, learn about training requirements, and search for job opportunities in social work on this web site.

www.careervoyages.gov/healthcare-main.cfm
This web site, by the U.S. Department of Labor, gives a useful overview of and statistics from the health care industry.

www.discovernursing.com
This web site offers information on nursing opportunities and salaries, as well as a search engine for programs and scholarships, videos on nursing, and more.

www.explorehealthcareers.org
Offers everything you want to know about a wide variety of health care careers, including complementary medicine and mental health.

www.nurse.com
If you're interested in a nursing career, this web site offers career profiles and information on a wide variety of nursing positions. Includes resources for student nurses as well.

Glossary

adoption a legal undertaking to create a parent-child relationship between people not related by blood

Alzheimer's disease a disease of the brain, where the memory and judgment gets worse, leading to dementia

complementary medicine a type of healing practiced by therapists who treat the person as a whole and try to restore the body's natural balance. Therapies include osteopathy, massage, and reflexology.

counseling listening to people's problems and helping them to resolve them in a structured way

court order a special ruling by a judge

database a collection of information, especially computer records

degenerate to get worse

detox short for detoxification, the process of removing toxins or poisons from the body

dexterity physical skill, especially of the hands

diagnose to identify a disease or condition by examining the symptoms

documentation paperwork or documents

empathize the ability to understand and engage with others' feelings

foster parents people who care for children and young people who have been removed from their biological parents

holistic treating as a whole

homeopath a therapist who uses homeopathy (the method of treating illness using a tiny amount of a drug that would normally produce symptoms similar to the effects of the illness)

hospice a home for people in care, especially terminally ill patients

labor the process of giving birth

manipulation treating manually

pediatrics the branch of medicine dealing with the care of infants and children

pharmaceutical industry the drug industry, or manufacture of medicines

postpartum depression feelings of extreme gloom following childbirth

prenatal happening before birth

prescription a document written by a health care professional such as a doctor or optometrist

probation a trial period; a court system that deals with offenders by placing them under the supervision of a probation officer

psychiatrist a doctor trained in treating various mental disorders

psychology the scientific study of all forms of human behavior

psychotherapist someone trained to help others in the problems of living by treating their mental well-being

referral someone transferred from the care of one health professional to another

reflexologist a therapist who uses reflexology (squeezing parts of the feet or hands for benefits elsewhere in the body)

rehabilitation helping a patient readapt to society

role play acting a role as part of a process of helping people recover from trauma or difficulties

schizophrenia mental illness characterized by deteriorating personality

sociology the study of human social behavior

surgeon a doctor who specializes in surgery

therapist someone who treats disorders or disease

ultrasound using ultrasonic waves in medical diagnosis and therapy

volunteer performed willingly, without being paid

welfare well-being; health and happiness

Index